# Unexpressed Emotions



Gino Lavayen

BookLeaf Publishing

Presentation by *BookLeaf Publishing*

Web: www.bookleafpub.com

E-mail: info@bookleafpub.com

ISBN: 9789357210645

First edition 2022

# DEDICATION

All my past, present, and promising future. My parents and friends (too many of you to name on here). To my doubters. To anyone who can relate and needs some form of comfort.

# Don't call me Mr. Nice Guy

First impressions,
They matter at first,
Consistency is the key to building stability,
but never assume a pattern can't take a turn,

I'm neither good or bad,
Whatever the in-between looks like,
That's where I sleep,
Sometimes I can't tell who's in control,

Every gentle smile,
Every warm hug,
Even my kind words,
All of it is real as much as I can cause pain,

It's never my intention to make you cry,
Apologies if I ever leave you bruised,
Please don't place me in high regard,
That way you won't be surprised when I make a mistake,

There's fear in me even when I take risk,
Underneath this strong persona lies a screaming child,

When all you hear is hope, doubt is only a few step behind,
As much as I can love hard, imagine how ugly my hate can be

# Smile my friend. It's not that serious.

I know it feels like the end of the world.
Like it's you against everyone else.
I got some news for you,
We've all been there,

Mom and dad had some hardships,
Your heroes struggled to be where they are,
we focus only on the destination,
Never understanding you have to move
mountains to make some noise,

It's okay to fail,
No shame in crying,
Admit when you're afraid,
Everything's temporary,

You say you're ready to give up,
Why do you laugh?
Why do you hope?
Why do you still love then say it's a wrap?

Take a walk with me,
Let it out,
Afterwards smile,

A moment's pain is nothing compared to the riches coming your way,

# She's Strong

Don't you worry about them,
Their annoyance will pass like everything else,
All this is a sign,
A sign that you're exactly where you need to be,

You're struggling,
You're thriving,
I know it ain't easy believe me,
Can't imagine how many times you wanted to
call it quits,

Put your make up on,
Buy that outfit you've had your eye on,
Let them stare,
That's the closest they'll get to having their way,

It'll be alright,
The odds are already in your favor,
Let him leave,
And watch him realize you were better off
without his toxicity

Be strong,
Be courageous,
Keep on smiling.
The sun shines brighter where you stand

# Kiss

I heard you said I'm a flirt,
You're not wrong,
Oh you say I'm like those guys,
Now we have ourselves a situation,

Not once did I mention taking you to bed,
Yes you caught me looking,
Just like I caught you smiling,
Let's not pretend this is innocent,

Get your facts straight,
These eyes were staring,
But not in the common area,
I never left them between your nose and chin,

We lock in and it's delicious,
Just like the movies,
Body on the wall,
Hands being where they need to be to close the distance,

You say it was only that one time,
Then I see you staring,
You see me smiling,

Looks like we're about to have another repeat of that same situation,

# Same mistake. Different name.

I was being nice,
You showed me your gratitude in the middle of the night,
Time passed and you wanted more than the tension,
On the day of my birthday, my bed was covered in my tears,

Brand new year for the both of us,
After hearing your pain, you invited me in for a passionate night,
Left notes under your door,
Next day your door wouldn't open even when the lights were on,

Spent all summer chatting,
Made it work until you developed issues,
Suddenly I'm like "every other guy",
Called it quits assuming the worst with no evidence,

Never been one for chasing,
Vibes were there after an introduction,

Came close to believing this could last,
The the back and forth left me emotionally damaged,

These tales don't end when there's always someone else,
The line gets blurry between a moment and a false promise,
Don't take it to heart,
Find comfort knowing it was you over anyone else,

# Proud Nerd

Oh I'm not ashamed,
I'll probably play video games until I die,
You won't have to wait until Halloween,
Next week I'll cosplay with everyone else,

Ever been to a comic book shop?,
You're missing out,
One visit will get you hooked,
There's something for everyone,

Enjoy role playing games?
Try dungeon and dragons,
Grab some snacks,
It's going to be a long night,

Free on the weekend?
Look up some anime,
You see ads all over the place,
Be part of a community that's loud and proud,

Look at my posters and you'll know I'm not hiding,
Listen to the excitement in my voice,
The figures displayed on my desk,
What can I say? It's a part of me I take pride in

# Dear Young Writer

The road to me is messy,
I'm sorry for that,
You don't deserve what's to come,
You wouldn't be me without the chain of events,

You were told to quit,
I'm your living proof,
That our hand still wields a pen like a weapon,
And the notebook is our shield,

Don't close up,
Even if they break your heart,
Because of them,
We're always at the store buying more pends and paper,

Let them hear your hidden voice,
Watch them be moved,
Watch as they demand more,
Watch as all this builds your character,

It get better,
Ignore their perception of you,
Mistakes are bound to happen,
Remember you lose when you stop trying,

# Dear Alcohol

I hate you,
I love you,
you bring the best in me,
when I should be at my best without you,

Thank you for the warm bodies at night,
Those deep conversations with strangers,
Memories I could never forget,
For feeling alive,

I need you and you know it,
There are worst outlets for me,
At least when numbness hits,
You tell me when enough is enough,

You're not my friend,
You're toxic,
You're addicting,
Encourage anything as long as it's done,

Flirtatious, fearless, determined, and joy,
He's me with your influence,
Don't you get it?
He's the reason you're not shattered in pieces

# One Mistake Doesn't Change me

How can you say you know me?
I don’t even know myself,
You think I can’t make the same decisions as
you?
I simply choose not too,

I’m me and don’t you forget it,
Everyone nowadays has something to prove,
What a joke,
Change doesn’t come fast enough because of it,

My morals are set,
Even those can be broken,
I’m one bad day away from being you,
Thinking about the possibility of it makes me
want to puke,

How can I learn without taking risks?
No I wasn’t manipulated or pressured,
Stop being dramatic,
I knew what I was doing,

For better or worse,

My journey continues as long as I draw breath,
I plan to evolve,
I aim to reach my full potential,

# Everything's Temporary

A broken heart will heal,
Don't take it personal,
That's just part of life,
We're running on a timeline,

If it ain't her,
It's someone else,
If it ain't that job,
You're one step closer to your dream,

It's not that serious,
It hurts now,
Smile anyways,
Don't let your enemies know you can bleed,

You only fail if you give up,
When you wake up know that you're winning,
Give yourself credit,
Others are one step away from falling,

See how you can benefit from it,
Everything has a lesson,
Stay ready,
Always show up,

# What is love?

I think about you when you're not around,
I pray for your health and fortune,
The reunion we're destined to have,
The memory we'll add to our shared moments,

Conversations to reflect on,
Their family becoming yours,
Invitations to celebrate our victories,
The risk of being vulnerable to the unknown,

A random act of kindness,
A soft kiss,
A warm hug,
Being seen with open mindedness instead of
assumptions,

It is dangerous,
One of the biggest motives to our actions,
It comes,
And it goes,

Nothing can prepare you for it,
But you hold on to it,
Like a dream worth fighting for,
It's easier to have than to keep,

# First step

My friends talk about hitting home run,
They made up their minds in under a minute,
That's where we differ,
Because you can't hit home run without making it to first base,

You wear your clothes like they were made for you,
Your laugh makes me want to laugh with you,
I can't break contact when I meet your eyes,
How do people miss out on the beginning stages of meeting someone new?

Wasn't there something I was supposed to do?
Can't think straight with you around,
Don't know how you did it,
But can you please keep me here with you a little longer?

A good time means nothing without good company,
Would you like to be my someone for tonight?
Can I be yours?
Especially if we can't promise each other tomorrow?

First step with me starts with your lips,
Thinking about kissing them again and again,
Making each one feel like it's our first time,
Anything after that is anyone's guess but it's worth it anyways,

# Speechless

I have food, clothes, and a roof over my head,
Anyone who says "not enough" is ungrateful,
To have more is considered a privilege,
But you darling would be a blessing,

I'm always looking forward to surprises,
Because in life almost nothing is brand new,
Just when I've given up,
You had to come around and give me a reality
check,

Sweetheart I was ready before you,
First date, first kiss, first gift,
No matter what you have in store for us,
I promise you have to catch up to me,

I've seen this movie a million times,
This time I'm a director,
Hope you like happy endings,
Those are the best kinds to end a story like ours,

I'm speechless,
This is not a dream,
Everything happens for a reason right?
Thank god for beauty in the unknown,

# Inner Thoughts

She's impossibly beautiful,
There's this feeling in my stomach I can't shake,
Is it too soon to ask her out?
What if I never see her again?

He's very handsome,
This feeling is captivating,
Too shy to put my thoughts into words,
I hope I don't scare him away,

I asked her out,
She said yes,
Asked me if this is a date,
Putting it all on the line by saying it is,

I told him it's a date,
I think we're both crazy,
Somehow I doubt there's room for regret,
Something about him feels reassuring,

It's midnight,
Wide awake thinking about her smile,
It's midnight,
Wide awake thinking about how much he made me laugh,

# Inner Thoughts (pt 2)

Things have been going great,
I'm at a point where her name equals a smile,
Her touch feels like the most secure location,
And her lips brings me a step closer to pure
happiness,

His name sets the mood right,
Patience does come with its rewards,
Having a hard time believing he exist,
Yet here he is providing his shoulder for me to
nap on,

She's into me and I'm left without words,
The more we grow the more fear builds up,
Like magic those thoughts disappear,
I doubt she has a reason to look the other way,

The other day be blessed me with a surprise,
I don't think he knows how much it meant to
me,
My friends are going to love him,
Hopefully his friends will feel the same way,

I think I'm ready,
Wonder what she'll say when I ask her,

I’m ready to take a step forward,
At this point he should already know my answer

# Does she know?

Do we believe what we want to believe?
A fantasy is more delicious than our reality,
We give in to what we want,
But never listen to that tiny voice telling us what we need,

You don't want him,
Admit it before it's too late,
His dirty secrets are not a mystery to you,
What are you so afraid of?

Does he look at you the way I try not to?
Can he keep you smiling longer than he pretends to love you?,
You're a queen,
The only one who doesn't see that is you,

Invest in you,
Stop burning money to look a certain way,
You're already a sight to behold,
Am I the only one who thinks this way?

Tell your story to set you free,
They will say you're weak,

But vulnerability is not a bad thing,
Don’t be afraid to endure it in the moment,

# Her Story

The city is quiet tonight,
It's past midnight,
My parents must be worried by now,
But I don't want to leave him yet,

"Babe?", he says,
"Yes?", I say,
"I can tell you're deep in thought. What's up?",
"Please don't take me home",

As if he read my mind,
Suddenly I can smell the ocean,
A lecture will likely come my way,
And it'll be worth the trouble,

Not a soul in sight,
Nature blessed us with her gifts tonight,
His warmth comforts me from the cold breeze,
If ever there were a picture moment, this is it,

An hour later, "Babe, you sure it's not too late?",
Under my breathe, "I always have energy for
you",
"What was that", he whispers,

Five minutes later, sleep takes me with an unbreakable smile,

# Dirty Thoughts At Night

One night you were too close,
Our lips were itches away,
Once we locked in,
Your body was pinned against the wall,

You looked sexy in that skirt,
Pink looks good on you,
Took everything in me not to stare,
Little did you know my lips almost bled trying to control myself,

That smile,
The way you giggle,
Every time we converse,
It's hard not to ask for more of you,

Lights on,
Perfect body,
Private room,
How many rounds can we go in one night?

Same dream different night,
No one knows,
Alcohol almost told you my secret,
You're dangerous to be around,

# Not Alike

I look forward to failure,
You're ready to call it quite when it gets tough,
I'm in love with the pressure,
It lets me know I'm on the right path,

Fail once,
Try again,
Fail Twice,
Keep going until you get it right,

Why let it define you?
It happens to the best of us,
This is just another cycle of life,
Don't let it stop you,

If it were easy we'd all be successful,
That's why I stand out,
Even when I bleed,
These legs keep moving forward,

Don't feel sorry for me
There's an endgame to this,
I plan to see this through,
See you at the top,

# Can I Take You Out to Dinner?

LA looks beautiful at night don't it?
So many sights to see,
So little time,
Why spend the evening alone at home?

Get up,
Netflix will still be there when you return,
Don't worry about the bills,
Problems can wait until tomorrow,

You hungry?
Tell me your favorite spot,
Matter of fact surprise me,
I got you,

You can say you're not interested,
but we know you're bluffing,
you won't regret it,
wear something nice,

It's my treat,
Be ready by seven,
I'll wait if I have to,
Don't expect to come home early

# Illusions

Let's not pretend living a lie isn't comforting,
Reality blows,
But like a drug,
The alternative sounds addicting,

Check this out,
You see her all the time,
You and her against the world is a dream come true,
Wouldn't it be nice had she said yes?

The crowd is on fire,
They're begging for another album,
What a high that would be,
Instead you're fighting to stay awake on a graveyard shift,

Family and friends couldn't be more proud,
You're all they talk about,
An inspiration that will carry on for generations,
Sadly you haven't found a reason to get out of bed,

Imagination is powerful,
Until you're forced to face the truth,

Careful not to drink too much of it,
It's a scary place when you feel like you've been robbed

www.ingramcontent.com/pod-product-compliance
Lightning Source LLC
Chambersburg PA
CBHW051753130826
49812CB00033B/1130
*9789357210645*